Noah's Ark
Original title: Die Arche Noah
Copyright © 1982 by Annette Betz Verlag im Verlag
Carl Ueberreuter, Vienna - Munich
English translation copyright © 1983 Hodder and Stoughton Limited

Library of Congress Cataloging-in-Publication Data
Fussenegger, Gertrud, 1912–
    Noah's ark.

    Translation of: Die Arche Noah.
    Summary: Retells the story of how Noah and the
animals survived the flood.
    1. Noah's ark—Juvenile literature.   2. Bible
stories, English—O.T.   Genesis.   [1. Noah's ark.
2. Bible stories—O.T.]   I. Fuchshuber, Annegert,
ill.   II. Title.
BS658.F8713 1987   222′.1109505   87-45153
ISBN 0-397-32241-0
ISBN 0-397-32242-9 (lib. bdg.)

Printed in Singapore. All rights reserved.
1 2 3 4 5 6 7 8 9 10
First American Edition

NOAH'S ARK

BY GERTRUD FUSSENEGGER

ILLUSTRATED BY ANNEGERT FUCHSHUBER

TRANSLATED BY ANTHEA BELL

J. B. LIPPINCOTT   NEW YORK

Long, long ago, in a far, distant land, there lived a man called Noah who was good and just, and believed in God.

Every evening when the sun was going down, Noah came out of his house, looked at the sun, and said, "Father in Heaven, I thank you for making the world so beautiful. Watch over us tonight and protect us from all evil!"

Then Noah went back into his house to join his wife and sons, locked the door, and slept peacefully.

Now why did Noah ask God to protect him and his family every evening? Was it storms he feared, or wild beasts?

No: Noah was not afraid of storms or wild beasts. He was afraid of his fellow men, because they were wicked. They lied and cheated and hurt one another. Brothers were enemies; sisters slandered sisters. The rich were proud and haughty, wasted their wealth, wore gold and precious stones, and would not give so much as a crust of bread to the poor. They beat defenseless people with whips and sticks. So Noah was afraid of his fellow men, and he prayed daily for God's protection.

God, who had made Man, was not pleased with his creation anymore.

For God had created men and women out of pure love, giving them bright eyes and sharp ears, clever hands, and mouths to speak and tell the truth.

But now God saw that people were using their eyes only to see what they could steal and their ears only to hear wicked words. They used their hands to hurt each other and their mouths to curse and tell lies.

God said to himself, "I will wipe men and women off the face of the earth." And he decided to send a great Flood, which would cover all the land.

No human beings were to be spared—except for Noah and his family.

So one night God woke Noah and spoke to him.

"Noah," he said, "listen to what I say. You must get up and rouse your sons, and you must all go out to the woods, where you are to build a great, tall vessel of good planks: an Ark with many cabins in it and a stout roof. You must make the Ark very strong and paint its seams with pitch to keep out the water. I am going to send a Flood to cover the whole earth, but you and your family will be saved."

And God said, "I will save the lives of the innocent animals as well, so you must take two of every kind of living creature into the Ark. And take food and water to last a long time. Make haste, Noah, for the Flood is coming soon!"

This was what God said to Noah.

Noah was amazed by God's words, but he got up at once and roused his sons, and they all set to work.

They took axes and saws and hammers, and went out to the woods, where they chose the tallest, strongest trees and cut them down. They chopped them up into planks, and then they began to build the Ark.

Soon word went round that Noah was at work on some great building. People came to watch. What was it going to be? A huge wooden house, or a tower, or a fortress?

Suddenly the watchers realized that the building was to be a ship. They laughed and laughed. Who ever heard of a ship on dry land? It was a ridiculous idea—only a fool would have thought of it! "Noah is a fool!" cried the people. They sang mocking songs and danced around the Ark.

But Noah took no notice. He gritted his teeth, and he went on building until the Ark was finished.

There it stood, just as God had told Noah to build it: vast and tall and almost black, because it was painted with pitch both inside and out.

Noah was tired after all his hard work, but he could not rest yet. He thought he still had the most difficult thing of all to do.

God wanted him to take two of every kind of animal living on earth into the Ark, but how was he to do that? How could he catch the fierce lions and shy gazelles, the terrible rhinoceroses and mighty elephants? How could he catch the birds of the air: the fast-flying swallows, or the bold eagles who build their nests high on the steep crags?

Noah did not know how he could ever carry out God's orders.

But then, one day, all the animals came of their own free will: tigers and lions and elephants, too. Timid birds came flying in, and the butterflies and bees and beetles flew with them. They came from far and wide, and they all went into the Ark.

Perhaps the animals felt that something strange was going to happen, and scented danger in the air. Perhaps they guessed that this great, black Ark was here to save them.

The day was much like any other day, except that the sunlight was stronger than usual and the air was heavier. Dark clouds were slowly forming. Then great drops of rain began to fall. It rained harder and harder, it rained all day long. And then it rained for a second day, and then a third.

At first, people were glad of the rain. "We shall have enough water at last!" they said. "All the wells will be full!"

But as time went by, they did not like the rain so much. Streams and rivers rose and burst their banks. Then Noah went into the Ark with his wife and his sons and his daughters-in-law, and waited to see what would happen.

And the Flood came.

Water surged up from the depths of the earth. The waves of the sea rose and crashed in breakers on the beach. Valleys became huge lakes, houses collapsed, bridges floated away. The people hastily packed up their most precious possessions: The rich packed their bags of gold and the poor their clothes and bedding, and they all fled to the hills and the mountains.

But many of them never reached those high places and were drowned in the Flood.

However, the water could not harm the Ark and the living creatures inside it.

The great, dark vessel stood where it was for a while, with the floodwaters washing around it, and then the waves lifted it and carried it away.

Man and beast, they sat in the dark inside and listened.

They felt the Ark turn and drift with the current; they heard the deep roar of the waves. Noah went around and gave out food and fodder. Sometimes he thought he heard pitiful wailing through the sides of the Ark.

He knew that by now the Flood had covered all the land. Even the last and strongest of the people, who had clung to the treetops or climbed mountain peaks, were washed away and drowned.

The Ark drifted on all alone, over an endless sea.

How much longer would the voyage last?

Noah did not know. He wondered how long he and his family and all the animals could live in the dark, cramped quarters of the Ark. The air was hot and heavy, and provisions were running out. Noah could hear the tigers snarling and the bears growling; the elephants were trampling, and the wolves were howling.

Lord God, thought Noah, when will you let us out of the Ark?

But Noah knew that first the water must go down and flow into the sea; it must seep away or dry up.

And Noah told himself that that would surely take a very long time.

"O God, Father in Heaven," prayed Noah in his heart, "help us and do not forget us!"

God had not forgotten Noah and all the other living creatures in the Ark.

God steered the Ark over the Flood until it came near a great mountain range, which would be the first thing to show above the waters when they went down. Indeed, the topmost peak was already above the water, and a few green things were beginning to grow there.

But Noah could not see them.

I will send out a raven, he thought. If the raven does not come back, I shall know that we are near land, and we can leave the Ark. But if he comes back, I shall know we must stay here.

So Noah sent out the raven, but the raven did not find land and came back again.

Meanwhile, the little island of land was growing larger. Other islands too were showing above the water.

Then Noah sent out another raven, but the second bird also failed to find land and came back.

Then Noah was sad and very much afraid. The air inside the Ark was almost unbearable by now, and the darkness was very gloomy. All but a little of the food was gone. The animals were bellowing with hunger, drumming their hoofs and paws against the cabin walls.

Noah's wife wept, and his sons and daughters-in-law were saying, "We might as well have stayed outside to drown with the others. We shall either stifle or starve to death in here!"

In his moment of greatest need, Noah thought: I will send out one more bird. So he took a dove and let her fly.

If she comes back too, we are lost, thought Noah. He watched her go as she disappeared over the horizon.

His heart sank when the dove came back only an hour later. But then he could hardly believe his eyes, for she was carrying an olive branch in her beak, and the branch was fresh and green.

Noah knew now that there was land not far from the Ark, and he knew that green things had begun to grow on the earth again. The olive trees were putting out shoots and would soon bear fruit. The flooded, barren earth would bring forth life again.

Joyfully, Noah showed his family the green olive branch.

And while they were all laughing and weeping for joy and hugging one another, the keel of the Ark grounded upon sand. They had come safely to harbor.

They opened the door and let out all the creatures, who had spent so long in the darkness of the Ark longing for fresh air and freedom.

The lions leaped out; the elephant waved his trunk and trumpeted aloud. Camels and gazelles trotted into the open air. Birds soared up, singing with delight. The mice and lizards, beetles and caterpillars, were scurrying and scrabbling and creeping and crawling, as they all made their way out to begin life again.

Noah's heart was full of thanks and praise as he stepped out onto dry land. "Father in Heaven, you have saved us!" he cried. "We bless your name! How wonderful you are!"

Then he built an altar and offered a sacrifice. God was pleased and said, "I promise I will never send such a great Flood again to destroy everything and everyone, even though people's hearts are wicked. As long as the earth remains, spring, summer, autumn, and winter will always come in their turn—the seeds will grow and the farmers will bring in the harvest.

"And you, Noah, and your family, because you have been true to me, will have more children, so that the earth will be filled with people once more."

And God set the many-colored rainbow in the sky as a sign of his promise to Noah.